"Tantlinger's chilling poetry, inspired by life/lies of a serial murderer, unfolds in the imagined voices of his victims, and the man himself, in a city reduced to ashes and rebuilt for him to bleed. The poems entice to try understanding this devil: what does he gain from such horror? In the end, after he is hanged and buried, the haunting last poem plants the idea: evil is more than one man and isn't easily destroyed."

—Linda D. Addison, award-winning author of "How to Recognize a Demon Has Become Your Friend" and HWA Lifetime Achievement Award winner

"In this morbidly creative and profound crime documentary, Sara Tantlinger delivers one of the best works of horror poetry I've read in years. What America's Ripper, HH Holmes, built with his creatively sick "murder castle" in 1890's Chicago, Tantlinger creates today with this book, rich with seductive language and unflinchingly exploratory in its multifaceted structure. It's brilliantly constructed to get inside your skull and pry apart your morbid fascination with life, death, perversion, avarice and murder, awakening you to the evil that hides in plain sight around us all. Readers will thrill to find themselves spilling down its terrifying trapdoors and careening down its greasy dark slides, until they find themselves imprisoned inside the black gloom of a deviant dungeon of nightmarish evil that they'll never be able to forget...or escape. An amazing autopsy of the unholy!"

—Michael Arnzen, Bram Stoker Award winning author of Grave Markings and Play Dead

"A fascinating and absolutely riveting journey into the life and times of one H.H. Holmes. Sara Tantlinger's powerful and vivid prose takes you into the depths of Holmes' dark universe and what you see will stay with you long after you've closed the book."

—Christina Sng, Bram Stoker Award winning author of A Collection of Nightmares

THE DEVIL'S DREAMLAND
POETRY INSPIRED BY H.H. HOLMES

BY SARA TANTLINGER

Published by Strangehouse Books
an imprint of Rooster Republic Press LLC
www.rooosterrepublicpress.com
roosterrepublicpress@gmail.com

Copyright © Sara Tantlinger
Cover Design by Nicholas Day, Don Noble
Edited by Nicholas Day
Interior Design – Don Noble

All rights reserved. No part of this book may be reproduced or transmitted in any form or by any means, electronic or mechanical, including photocopying, recording, or by any information storage and retrieval system, without the written consent of the publisher, except where permitted by law.
Printed in the USA.

Find our catalog at
www.roosterrepublicpress.com

Author's Note: On Writing H.H. Holmes

An enigma. That's where we start when it comes to Herman W. Mudgett, better known as H.H. Holmes, though he would take on other names throughout the term of his nefarious career. Most of what we think we know about Holmes is the result of unreliable sources, newspapers embellishing details to sensationalize stories (ha, sound familiar?), and of course the fact that Holmes was an amazing liar. Even his handwritten prison memoir was deeply misleading. He wrote it in hopes of gaining public sympathy as he claimed innocence for some rather ghastly murders. When he did write a "confession," he wrote of murdering people who were in fact proven alive. So to attempt to understand Holmes' mind is not an easy feat, but it sure is interesting to try.

This is where the fun, for me at least, came into play during the creation of this collection. I read so many resources about Holmes over the past several months, watched documentaries, listened to podcasts that discussed the man...the information was overwhelming, often contradictory, and always a good source for writing fodder.

If you're curious to read more of the facts about Holmes, take a look through the many sources Adam Selzer has compiled over the years, such as *The True History of the White City Devil*. Other favorite sources, that perhaps embellish a bit more and have fun with the details like I did, are Erik Larson's *The Devil in the White City* and Harold Schechter's *Depraved*. I also had a blast reading the legendary Robert Bloch's *American Gothic* novel, which he based on Holmes and the infamous "Murder Castle."

The following poems are not a history lesson, but they were certainly inspired by accounts and tales that spawned from the misdeeds of one Dr. H.H. Holmes. Both fact and speculation intertwine here, thus what follows is the version of the madman who has been living inside my head for the past year.

When it comes to Holmes, there's so much room for everyone to play. He is a mystery belonging to no one, yet we keep coming back to read more about him, to try and figure out just what was happening inside that twisted mind. So come with me, if you will, to the devil's dreamland – there's plenty of room for everyone in the cellar.

Table of Contents

11	Metamorphosis
Beginnings	
15	The Bloodletting of a New Century
16	Womb of Madness
17	Innocence like Birdsong
18	Anatomy Lesson
19	Push
20	Inaugural Dismemberment
21	The Dissection Doctor
22	The First Wife: Clara
23	In High Demand
24	Mistress
25	The Tenant
26	Earthworms
27	Chasing the Hunger
Chicago: Part I	
31	The Great Chicago Fire
33	Blood Clot Passenger
34	Englewood
35	The Second Wife: Myrta
36	Mimic
37	Lips Bitten Raw
39	Chloroform
40	Dark Appetites
41	Accomplice
42	Strabismus
43	The Kiln
45	Holmes vs. The Ripper, Part I
46	Machinist
47	Holmes vs. The Ripper, Part II
48	Mr. and Mrs. Connor
49	Dear Julia
50	Nothing Owed
51	Silence on the Morning After
52	The Articulator
53	The Keeley Institute
55	Angel
56	Emeline
58	Endgame
59	The Vault
60	Compendium of Dying Breaths
Chicago: Part II	
63	The Devil's Dreamland
65	Shades of Wild Plum
66	World's Columbian Exposition
68	Minnie
69	Performance Piece
70	Sisters

71	Scarlet Siege
72	In the Castle's Heart, You Die
74	Incinerate
75	The Darkness Swallows Your Prayers
76	Celestial
77	Serenade to a Corpse
78	Curtain Call

Pursuit

81	One Last Scheme
82	Georgiana
83	Dead Girls and Money Schemes
84	When the Inferno Begins, I Light it Myself
85	Blood Money
86	No Entry, No Exit
87	Oversight
88	Hollow
89	Imbibe
91	Putrefaction
92	Known Decay
93	Pawns
95	Howard Pitezel
97	Alice and Nellie Pitezel
98	Sisters in Shallow Graves
99	Panic, Amnesia, and a Madman's Game

Caught

103	Moyamensing Prison
104	Earned Conviction
106	Evidence
107	Daydreams from a Jail Cell
108	Deliverance
109	Yours, H.H. Holmes
110	Three Wives Dressed in Black
111	The Undeath of Malevolence
112	Kymographion
113	Satanical Metamorphose
114	Villain Viscera
115	To Dream in Darkness
116	The Hanging
118	Metempsychosis
119	Unblessed Excavation

"Now this is the point. You fancy me mad. Madmen know nothing. But you should have seen me. You should have seen how wisely I proceeded --with what caution --with what foresight --with what dissimulation I went to work!"

-Edgar Allan Poe, "The Tell-Tale Heart"

Metamorphosis

I am
Herman Webster Mudgett (what's real, doesn't sound real, does it?)
raised by a mother's constant prayer,
hell-bound on that first metallic
tang of religion
ingrained deep into my flesh
by a father's frequent use of a rod
constant and unsparing
but pity me not,
for this is how I learned
love and violence swelter together
into one enflamed desire

I am
Dr. Henry Howard Holmes (better now? better)
the doctor is in, far away from a young wife and son,
but I will take other wives and mistresses
one who will bare another child
spreading the devil in my DNA onward
because parasitical intents are not created
for containment,
I discover my enlightened self in Chicago,
buildings clad in snowy stucco
lamplights casting angelic glows onto streets,
I can see why they call this the White City,
my footsteps fall like a sooty, black rain
dark as a plague
promising practiced, surgical hands to unfold
the city's ribs, pluck out its heart
squeeze meaty thumps of dying beats
over everything in a rhythm of blood songs

I am
H.H. Holmes (do you know me yet?)
standing at the precipice of life,
my demon inside me, but I name him friend
later, he names my building
the Murder Castle
with its trap doors, secret passages,
never fully finished in its construction,
but the walls are always listening
as I remove sutures of skin from those
in my employment

I am
your American serial killer, wrapped up
in 19th century shreds of screaming women
trapped behind soundproof walls
where ribbon-soaked memories
drip down into soil,
later, within scrawled prison memoirs,
I will articulate contradictions
confess to murders of those still living
as people falsify accounts of things untrue
because you will never know what it is like
to be born with the Evil One inside you

here in prison my face grows gaunt,
my eyes grim
I am
someone you will never truly know

I am
the worst kind of thing you could ever find
as you crawl your way across a hotel floor
fall down a sliding trapdoor into a room
filled with acid bottles, a stretching rack,
cleaned up skeletons
forever locked in a purgatory grin

I am
your timeless Devil
you will never know me, yet
I am
everywhere

Beginnings

"That the first years of my life were different from those of any other ordinary country-bred boy, I have no reason to think."

–Herman W. Mudgett (alias H.H. Holmes), *Holmes' Own Story*, 1895

The Bloodletting of a New Century

I want to tell you what I was supposed to be.

Destined to bring forth glory,
new century, new generation
brimming with the shine of bright
crimson rays across my horizon,

dying years of the 1800s,
caught between the old and new world
should have birthed
beautiful energy and ideas,
inventions, art, literature, science…

Instead, my fading dusk birthed a monster.

I should have been remembered
for gas lights and photographs,
moving pictures and recording sound,
the sapling growth
of telephones and automobiles.

Instead, I am complicit,
my forensics not quite
capable of conviction,
my science cannot
determine whose bones
lived and died inside
Holmes' basement,
a few more years
and I could have unraveled
the mystery,

but it's like he knew—
he knew this was the last
opportunity to be wild and bloody,
to capture enigma
dissect its chained-up body
on a cold metal slab.

I want to tell you what I was supposed to be,
but instead I am going to show you
the demon I created.

Womb of Madness

He is quiet inside of me
as if dreaming
as if contemplating

idyllically noiseless
the baby, my husband, our village.

The hushed air is too much,
I long for someone
to sneeze, whisper, scream.

I talk to myself
and to the wildflowers,
to the cows
and to my son

nestled deep within my body
dreaming, contemplating.

I swallow more quiet
whisper a prayer
to my silent God.

We will name him Herman
I hope he laughs loudly,
tells me secrets, captures fireflies
with gentle hands.

But when I sleep, with my fingers
steeped over my swollen belly
during the muteness of night
I dream of falling into warmth,
metallic and thick.

I do not fear the blood,
even as it drowns me,
madness wails
when the baby claws his way out.

I am grateful for the noise.

Innocence like Birdsong

They say if a feather falls
in front of you
when no birds are around

it is a gift from your guardian angel.

What do they say when
a young boy harvests
crow skulls

like secret treasure beneath his bed?

The bluebirds and robins,
finches and cardinals,
are not singing outside your window.

Their trills are warnings

to beware the dissector
who lives beyond this door
to not confuse guardian angels

with preadolescent demons.

Anatomy Lesson

Skeleton grin
bones outstretched
teeth ready to chatter,
as if to say,
give us a hug, dear Herman

Viscera in cloudy bottles
surrounding boy and carcass
diseased and tempting,
as if to say,
take off the lid, dear Herman
touch me, taste me

Push

The abandoned house loomed, grisly in its charm, seductive in its nature, but if nature is to reclaim what has been abandoned, then perhaps seductive charm can never be anything other than grisly. But these are not the thoughts of the two boys sneaking up decaying stairs, inhaling the grime, letting it settle deep in their lungs like a dusty kiss. Just children joking in the dirt, playing cops and robbers, but both are stealing away memories of this decayed magic, of this haunted emptiness. They will say the older boy, Tom, died from a fall, from something inevitably tragic because structures break in abandoned houses, they collapse and you tumble down the stairs, through the floor, and you just simply fall, simply shatter, simply die as the younger boy watches, those cold blue eyes, unblinking. His hands never once tremble.

Inaugural Dismemberment

Salamanders and frogs at first,
blinking amphibian eyes
slow, weary
before he scoops them up
strokes slender bodies

slices through soft bellies.

Rabbits, stray cats,
hungry dogs,
too slow, too trusting
before his young hands
wrap around in a stranglehold

dissecting the living, until they live no more.

Learning how to disable life
without completely killing it,
he does not know this yet,
but it won't be much different later
when he replaces animals with human bodies,
when he arranges a woman on his slab
instead of a yowling cat in the family cellar

how the women will fight
aim to scratch out his eyes,

he does not know yet
how animals won't haunt him,
won't come back when he steals
paws as keepsakes,

but the women,
whose clothes he will someday keep
hanging like slim ghosts
from his closet
will come back when he weaves
his dreamland,
will come back blinking slow
amphibian blackness
in place of their own, dead eyes.

The Dissection Doctor

In all my years of taking on apprentices
never has one been as excitable
as young Herman Mudgett, deliciously eager

    never has one craved to spend so much time
    in the dissection room

he understands deeply,
intimately
the gluttonous need to slice

    to peel back skin and examine sinewy
    inner workings of human cadavers

In all my years of sawing, cutting, scraping
at the oozing husk of a dead body,
I've never seen a man smile

    as he severs the body
    as he plunges hands deep inside

Inhaling the embalming chemicals
caressing the dead, withered organs,
his eyes alight, deliciously eager

The First Wife: Clara

Intelligent, well-spoken,
in possession of good manners,
pretty, young, devoted
properly Victorian,
perhaps he loved you once
the way society deemed necessary,

but darling Clara,
if only you knew
how heartache will arrive
like October-blown leaves
scattering in a chilled wind,
dry, shriveled, ready to crunch
beneath a footstep
just like your heart is,

your Herman, your husband
how he asserts promises
to you and the baby
how he proclaims love,
but sometimes love is not enough,
don't you see how the convulsions
wracking your body
are warnings from your bones,
your veins, your entire being
to run, to run, to run

how the bromide he delivers
to your bedside table, your "cure,"
breaks your face out with angry,
red splotches, breaks his face
out into nothing but pity stares

when he leaves and you feel broken,
when you have your head resting
on your father's knee, and the baby
nestled on your lap,
when you redefine love on your own terms
you can redefine your life
because at least, and you will learn
years from now,
at least he leaves you alive
at least he leaves you alive

In High Demand

The first time he steals a body,
young Mudgett is still in medical school,
they tell him this is part of the process
to learn more about dissections,
how the body functioned
between life and death,
grave digging for the sake of science

thieves, but not killers,
his colleagues explain
on a murderously hot night
where even the witching hour
cools down to a mere summer swelter,

an old cemetery awaits them,
wilting grass blades
sea of white crosses
surrounding the outer perimeter
like small sharks in a murky ocean,
two shovels protrude upward
staked through piles of disturbed earth

doctors raiding graveyards
protectors of life
robbing the dead of their eternal
resting beds because demand is high,
and they must have bodies

the first time he steals a corpse,
digs it up, breathes in the two-day-old
fetid stench of decomposing flesh,
he realizes the potential of the market involved,
realizes he could find his own ways
to meet the demand of body-hungry doctors

a hunger of his own grows deep
within the grottos of his calm heart,
hunger for money and authority
hunger for a moment where he could
witness the last stuttering blinks
twitching through a person
before snuffing out their lively pain

Mistress

He finds me in the winter
when the air is arctic-flavored
yet when he smiles,
I find warmth in those lips
taste the petals of spring
blooming on his tongue,
swallow his saliva
like rainwater

The Tenant

He is going to kill us all – this man I let stay
within the walls of my boardinghouse

Young medical student, what do you keep
beneath the bed where I must sweep?

Constant reek of chemicals, experiments,
he calls them, all for school, he claims

Poison goop, foul odors, leaking between
the floorboards like jellied garbage

Young medical student, what do you keep
beneath the bed where I must sweep?

He has turned the room into a lab, test tubes,
amber fluids, sick eagerness to work on dissections

The way he discusses such things at the dinner table
flirts with my daughter despite his wedding band

Young medical student, what do you keep
beneath the bed where I must sweep?

I cannot take the vulgar stench any longer,
so I wait until he goes to his classes this day

My broom in hand, I move toward the dark object
beneath his bed, the source of such nauseous smells

Down on one knee, I swoop the heaviness out,
it nearly rolls across the floor, dead weight

Young medical student, what do you keep
beneath the bed where I must sweep?

Tiny and cold, a blue-green bruised shade
long, jagged cuts across the chest and belly

I don't remember if I ever stop screaming
at my tenant's dissection project

I sweep it back, wondering whose baby
the young doctor had stored beneath his bed?

Earthworms

If you are searching for someone
to look you deep in the eyes
tell you gorgeous fabrications
there is a young doctor
down the road,
by the name of Mudgett
who carefully sidesteps earthworms
after the rain has fallen
vigilant not to squish their bodies,
squelch them into decorative guts
beneath his polished shoes

    yet he carries a skull fragment
    inside his jacket pocket
    a bit of dried lung
    inside a small, amber jar

he blows off debts,
does not pay rent
charms women, breaks them
misleads anyone into
swine-like schemes for money
loves the aroma
of embalming chemicals
in the fresh, dewy morning

    but he does not step
    on the earthworms
    helpless, crawling
    silently pleading
    for their lives

Chasing the Hunger

Everyone is starving here,
starving everywhere.

When I cannot stand the screams,
nor the way madness bleeds
deep into my own brain
from the screeches of those kept
behind tomb-cold walls
within Norristown Asylum,
I pace outside and ask
the Philadelphia moon
if she will satisfy my growing hunger,

tonight she does not
tomorrow she will not.

Everyone is talking here,
inside Norristown, inside my head.

I did not want this job
of madmen keeper, and after
a few days, I leave.
Hunger still rolls restless
within my churning mind,
ticking out ideas along
with the clacking of a train,

I can't stop thinking about
a brief visit I once took
to a city of allure, a city that once
died down to charred, ashen strips
after the great conflagration,

a city that rebuilt itself up
reaching for clouds and sun
skyward into the evolving world,
gleamingly pure in the daytime
wretched as sin during the night,
a balance I am hungering
to slide myself between.

Chicago – the delicious
taste of her in my thoughts,
opportunities abound,
a new beginning, new name

the train juts onward to Springfield,
so do my options,
because at last I realize I am no longer
running from asylums or mediocre jobs,
I am chasing after something greater,
an appetite aching beyond food, beyond money.

When I sign the registry to prove myself
a medical man,
the clicking in my brain holds tight
as the train tracks.

I amputate Herman Webster Mudgett from my identity,
sacrifice slices of soul back to the ravenous moon
that used to hang above the asylum in Philadelphia.

I sign the registry,
my new life to unfold
the book forever showing the name
Of *Dr. H. H. Holmes.*

Chicago: Part I

"Later, like the man-eating tiger of the tropical jungle, whose appetite for blood has once been aroused, I roamed about the world seeking whom I could destroy."

–Herman W. Mudgett (alias H.H. Holmes), *Holmes' Own Story*, 1895

The Great Chicago Fire of 1871

Conflagration, I am named,
but am I accident? Arson?
The work of a vengeful God?

I am soot and grit
the American dream
turned to charcoal death.

They built a city of tinder,
kindling for oceanic fire
hissing across the river,
consuming everything
as if the sun dripped flames
down in the middle of the night
smothering out Chicago's heart,
leaving only a blackened husk.

My citizens will spend so long
recreating my scorched coffin
into something habitable,
they will bleed hearts of phoenixes
into my soil, regrow me
make me rise,
so I rise,
so does death.

He is only ten when I am murdered,
when I birth smoke and ash.

They rebuild me and I become
the Great White City,
fit for a Great White Shark
of a human being.

Here, where my streets
are sewers,
where my people
are rats,
blood with money,

that ten-year-old grows up,
comes sniffing out that blood-money,
like rich, scarlet honey nectar
for his surgical hands to wrap around,
squeeze, lap it up,

stain the White City
with splattered carnage.

I no longer need a doctor to repair
damaged veins of restoration,
but the train whistles a warning,
it is too late.

He is coming,
he is here.

Blood Clot Passenger

1886, late summer, early morning
a man steps off a train
thirty-five years old, five foot eight
blue eyes
striking against
miasmic city filth
striking against
his well-dressed body

hearses roll by, iron-clad wheels rattling,
urging city rats to scamper
past bluebottle flies
hovering over animal corpses
littering over city streets
like masses on an artery

a man walks through the city
as summer rots
locomotive steam pluming upward,
conjoining with polluted clouds,
soot and smoke
thickening a blockage from the sun

1886, late summer, early morning
a man steps off a train,
the clot breaks free, travels through
Chicago's body,
this dark-mustached swindler,
this charmer who pied the snakes
swallowed them whole,

emits musical poison from his throat
walks past death without blinking
thirty-five years old, five foot eight
blue eyes
hungering over
the sight of maggots
wondering how squirming larvae
would look
inside the body of the pretty woman
he had sat next to on the train.

Englewood

At the corner of Wallace and Sixty-third,
within a booming business district
old widow, lonely widow
struggles to keep her late husband's pharmacy afloat

At the corner of Wallace and Sixty-third,
a young doctor charms the widow
suave as a serpent about to sink fangs into prey,
purchasing the store on promised payments,
money that she will never see

At the corner of Wallace and Sixty-third,
a gold-lettered name hangs outside the entranceway,
H.H. Holmes – new proprietor,
the men call him respectable, admirable even,
the women blink behind their veils, offer smiles

the old widow is never seen or heard from again

The Second Wife: Myrta

Holmes "marries" his second wife, Myrta Belknap, around 1886 (he's still legally married to Clara, though)

Young and lush,
Aryan in her features
needy, wanting,
desperate for courtship,

this is how I like them
oh, god yes, vulnerable,
what a beautiful word
a delectable ideal

even when I break
the rules of society's
standards for courting,
she falls into me so sweetly
she only ever whispers,
yesyesyes

Mimic
Myrta's great-uncle, Jonathan Belknap, comes to visit the newlyweds

There is something off,
    wrong,
        broken
about the man my niece calls husband
too much charm, too gracious, too blue in the eyes
intensity should not arrive bright as a sparrow
flapping hypnotizing wings in the shape of twisted
words that capture,
    seduce,
        break
a person's willpower to powder beneath a beak,
but my dear Myrta is persuaded, is mistaking
the mouth for a smile instead of seeing this
blood-feathered cannibal cardinal
who stinks the place up with copper lies;

he devours flesh to peck out the money
one may be in possession of, and deep beneath
pretty plumage awaits an intrinsic hunger
nibbling through muscles,
    tendons,
        nerves,
wringing out life until willpower depletes.

How do you pin the charmer down?

We must open him up, dissever his smile
find a trace of humanity hiding inside the gizzard,
I find nothing, only a perverse flicker
decrying morality as lackluster guidelines
made to be broken beneath the ice of his stare.

Later we will call this a malady, lack of a moral compass.
Later we will call this a perfect mirror, stunning reproduction
of someone's ability to reflect, mimic a personality.
Later we will call this… *psychopath.*

Lips Bitten Raw

She stays quiet
as her husband flirts
summons a blush
to the face of each attractive
young woman visiting the store

She bites her lip
using the taste of blood
as a reminder
she has a good life, a secure life

When the beautiful lady
laughs, loud and musical
from the front of the store
Dr. Holmes slightly brushes
a gloved finger over
the stranger's hand

Myrta bites her lip
bleeds violence
thinks maybe her husband
has been a mirage
all this time

Still, he flirts
later, they fight
his temper disintegrates
the once warm smile
beneath his mustache

He yells,
she bleeds,
each metallic drop
inside her mouth
is a reminder
you have a good life, a secure life

She does not dare
talk back to the red drops,
does not dare say,
well maybe I deserve
a better life

He shouts again
she bleeds again

her palms cupping
the slight swell
of a nauseous stomach
and what about the baby,
she asks,
what about the baby?

Chloroform

"Erikson," the thin lips say, his tone calm, gentle even. All the world's charm living inside that voice—
    poised, a snake ready to strike.

"My good man, if you would be so kind." He points to the chloroform behind me, tucked neatly in its bed on the shelf.

"That's the ninth time this week…" I say, my fingertips hesitating to move from the desk to the little colorless bottles of sweet-smelling medication. "What are you using all of this for? I can't sell you anymore unless you tell me."

His blue eyes sparkle, capture the dusty light of mid-afternoon. "I *am* a doctor, Erikson. I perform scientific experiments, you see."

His voice calm, gentle still,
    all the world's charm, all the world's snakes.

I sell him the drug again, again, again. This unpredictable, potent thing. An anesthetic from war times that has little need being bought in gulping quantities, but I am unsettled, undecided how to handle the blue-eyed viper slithering at my cash register.

Dr. Holmes returns next week, pacing my store, as if we both don't know what he wants. The irises are a little duller, a little more blank.

"How are your experiments, doctor?"

His blue eyes blink the way a sleepy, carnivorous reptile's would. Hungry. Confused.

"Experiments? I'm not conducting any experiments."

The voice calm, gentle almost,
    all the world's charm…

Dark Appetites

Myrta does not live here anymore
second wife, second baby,
I will keep them alive
but away from me
I will keep my spawn
out of curiosity

What will baby Lucy grow up to be?
What of the son I left behind in the east?

I wonder if their appetites
will grow as dark as mine
because I have been thinking,
worrying,
unable to deny
the gurgling, frothy hunger
spreading low in my belly
craving to hurt, to maim,
to watch light exit the eyes

I tell myself I am in control
building a palace for depravity
where my appetites and needs
can come play together
has been my plan all along,
I tell myself I am not a minion
serving a darker force who seethes,
whispers within my cerebrum
controlling my autonomy

a protrusion swells
beneath my scalp
cocking my bowler hat
slightly sideways,
when the welt
talks to me at night, it plants images
deep inside my head
showing me how to construct fantasy,
showing me blueprints
for a castle of the damned

Accomplice

With every good madman, comes a coconspirator,
or perhaps the madman creates something else

Take the monster within Dr. Frankenstein,
the humanity within his creature

Take the insatiable thirst of Dracula
and his bug-eating Renfield,
both consuming life-forces
because the answer is always blood

Blood as food, as drink
as a token from worshipper
to master,

for Holmes, along comes a carpenter
named Ben Pitezel
kind of a drunk
kind of loves his wife
and five children

easy to manipulate, simple-minded
enough to keep around
something akin to trust blossoms
between the two schemers

there will be an extent
to how far this bends,
to how far the boundaries
can twist, contort,
slither between the men

From this, the downfall
starts to steadily drip,
from this,
will come a reckoning.

Strabismus

Cold blue eyes,
    a cross-eyed misalignment
hue becomes lost
inside shadows of melancholy

Dark as a raven's,
    but no seeing or dreaming
one straight ahead, on you
the other rolling back, remembering

Her muffled scream
    a body convulsing
wrought upon the basement's floor,
cold blue eyes glimmer

You almost mistake this
    for a sign of humanity
but it is instead lust for death
a cross-eyed blink of wickedness

The Kiln

At night after the stores close
after stars attempt to blink
between ashen clouds,
the strange doctor
builds something,

something hungry inside
crooked architecture,
atrociously macabre.

What's in his basement?

Chicago swallows starlight,
the plague of a man
stays down below the earth.

What's in his basement?

He says, goodnight tenants,
goodwife wife,
goodnight mistress,
and hello to the fire light

where he sits like a pyro-hungry
piranha, listening to colorless flames—
an invisible reaper
instructing,
    seducing,
slithering
deep inside the doctor man.

He unbuttons his shirt,
holds his arms out wide
embracing his monstrosity
made from ruddy bricks,

and what is it there, inside his basement?

Heat emits from a cavernous mouth
blistering enough to melt iron
inside brick jaws.

Is this man the Devil or a minion,
trading flesh for secrets?
The kiln sings for him

crude oil mouth
mating with death,
delivering steam and atoms
from the ashes inside its belly.

Not even bones remain,
just a man's coat
hanging upstairs in the parlor,
just a woman's dress in her trunk
worn only by ghosts now,

bodies without skin,
without skeletons,
flaking bits of dust
tarred, human husks

in the doctor's basement,
in the Devil's kiln.

What else is he
building in there?

Holmes vs. The Ripper, Part I

November 1888,
cold metallic tang of blood
billows up in the atmosphere
hovering, haunting
crimson pollution in Victorian streets.

Slightly after the witching hour
a woman cries, "murder!"
Violence is nothing new here,
neighbors turn away, shut their ears
slicing off sound as he slices off
a woman's breasts.

Around 10:45am,
a landlord goes to collect rent
Mary Kelly's is overdue,
she doesn't open the door
blood smears the broken window.

Mary Kelly is nothing more
than a gumbo-stewed organ soup
scarlet flesh pile, skinned down,
inhumanly carved up on the bed
a massacre of mutilation.

There will come a debate after this,
was she truly the Ripper's last?
Are the following Whitechapel murders
his or someone else's?

At this stillborn, chilled moment
Jack remains the most brutal
servant of the Devil.

At this stillborn, chilled moment
H.H. Holmes hears
backward whispers slithering
into his small ears

You can do better
You can do better

Machinist

Within dark basement rot
he labors,
precision is important

Within dark basement rot
he hides the body—
skeleton from the waist up,
stripped skin hanging off bones
like mushed meat on a rack

lower limbs thick with flesh,
half-carcass, half-man
dismemberment flavors the air
seedy zest of blood and bile

Within dark basement rot
he labors,
practice and precision

perfection formed
by the taste of decay

Holmes vs. The Ripper, Part II

Dr. Holmes folds down the morning paper,
putting away the gooey mess of Jack.

The Ripper had been sloppy,
sexually exalted by thrusting
his hands inside of women,
tearing them inside out
like a blood-horny animal
     savage and visceral.

Dr. Holmes straightens the ink on his desk
brushes the lint from his trousers
organizes his files in a slow, neat order.

His workers are building,
adding new passages, staircases,
chambers, chutes, doorways
to his home, his workplace,
his castle where he envisions
beautiful dissections
     of beautiful women.

The Ripper had been sloppy
but Holmes will be precise,
careful with his slaughter
his experiments,
clean and quiet
the way love and butchery
     ought to be.

Mr. and Mrs. Connor (Ned and Julia)

Take a resentful marriage
add a pinch of angry silence
a dash of violent quarrels
and one night where the couple
tries to make amends
between faded sheets

One stillborn baby
is served up
adding heaps of strain
pints of blood
a recipe for misfortune

Take a fresh start in Chicago
where the dashing man
with a monstrosity of a building
offers a well-paying job
to manage the jewelry shop

where they have a healthy baby now, Pearl,
barely two years old,
where a purposefully oblivious
husbands turns an eye
to the charm of the young doctor
to the smile he extracts from the wife

a recipe for misfortune

Dear Julia

She is striking
so tall,
taller than me

chestnut hair pinned back
eyes green as fresh sea foam
exquisitely bright

the taste of mistress
is not foreign to my tongue,

but her independence is
her refusal of meekness,
she does not submit
to her toad of a husband

refreshing strength
draws me in,
she lays across scarlet sheets
slipping deeper under my skin
into my head

she knows what she wants,
so do I.

Nothing Owed

I will not explain myself
I owe no defense here

You can try hard
to slip fingers
between my lips,
pinch an explanation
with your nails
unravel it like tugging
a ribbon from a corset,

but I will explain nothing.

Swallow your judgment down
choke on it
because this body is mine
these hands, these legs
the curve of my lips
the ache of my heart

all belong to me,
and if my belly growls
in hunger of an ambitious man
instead of my trite husband

if I pad away at night,
quiet as a hunting cat,
curling into the doctor's arms

it is no concern of yours.

Silence on the Morning After
Christmas Eve, 1891

Sometimes I get ahead of my own game, sometimes people do not play the roles they are meant to. Dear Julia, I nearly loved you and dear Julia, you've gone too far – should have stayed with Ned, should have stayed married, should not have come tapping on my office door, dressed in raven black, hands folded over your stomach telling me what is *growing* in there, what we have planted...

When I promised marriage in return, you consumed the lie, and I thought you were smarter than this, but love terrorizes competent thought processes, doesn't it? Dear Julia, I already have burdens in the shape of children and you have Pearl, we cannot have another, you see? We cannot disintegrate ourselves into any more pieces, any more shreds of evidence even if they arrive in the form of crying babies...

My Holmes, what do you ask of me?

The procedure is simple. I have done this before.

I cannot get Pearl to sleep. She is too excited. It is Christmas Eve, after all.

Leave it to me, dearest Julia, meet me down in the basement. Forget your hesitance, your worries, your doctor is here to take care of all. And she goes, and I go, creeping into Pearl's bedroom, and she fakes sleep at the sight of me, the rag in my hand melds perfectly around her tiny mouth, inhale it deep, enter a real sleep, and it does not take much chloroform to send the small child into an embrace of the abyss – quiet now, quiet forever.

Dear Julia, lay on the table, and it takes more chloroform to relax her muscles, my tall buxom girl, my mistress who wanted too much, and oh, Julia, you look lovely as your eyes roll back, then close, as your steel grip on my cuff loosens, and my own arousal heats up as your heels beat madly on the slab, as you try to fight, struggle, fade away into stuttering darkness...

There now, all quiet my dear, my Julia, yes, rest now, forever – and perhaps in your death sleep you have married me at last. Yes, quiet now, Merry Christmas.

The Articulator

Articulation, not of words
not of the tongue

My mastery educates
stripping the flesh
from your loved one's carcass,

how to arrange bones
back into complete skeletons
for schools and medicine,
it is just business, my friend.

When the good doctor invites me
into his building of many rooms,
I am not alarmed at first

by the dead woman
on the table
because she is money
on the table;

he has already begun
some articulation
of his own.

A fouled up attempt
of dissected slivers,
meat ribbons flayed out
like remains of a tattered rabbit
that had spent too much time
gripped within a hound's jagged mouth.

Her ruined face is serrated, split skin
rolled and peeled back
like sticking thumbs into an orange,
juicing it dry and shedding layers
apart into unspooled gore

This ripped up corpse, these pieces
of a woman, paid for,
sold for even more

it is just business,
my friend.

The Keeley Institute

"Benjamin Pitezel?"

I nod as my name flows
from the delicate lips,
sensual and pink,
of the beautiful creature
sitting at the reception desk

They say the Keeley Institute
houses the "gold cure"
for alcoholism,
but her hair is so sunbeam yellow
that I wonder if she is the cure?

The treatment is noted as humane,
but I don't know what
loiters within the medicine they inject
other than the bichloride of gold,
the rest remains a mystery

There are whispers of ammonia,
alcohol, perhaps,
others think willow bark, atropine,
strychnine
morphine,

I don't know what dwells inside me,
liquids reflecting red, white, blue tonics,
a melted American flag waving
soothing stripes beneath my skin,
lessening the raging, aching need
to imbibe copiously, catatonically

And maybe this is therapeutic,
I fade in and out, unsure when I sleep,
when I am awake,
keep spotting glimpses of yellow hair,
easy smile, curved lips

She tells me I need to get better
for my wife, for my kids
my girls and little Howard,
my growing family

I tell myself I need to get better
for Mr. Holmes and his plan

The promise of riches awaiting,
if we can carry it out
if he keeps me alive

Angel

Benjamin Pitezel returns from the Keeley Institute, initially sober and doing well, but this will not last…

Doc, I saw a real life angel there
between the meetings, pills,
punishments

young and blonde and fresh
beautiful mouth
beautiful words

comforting angel,
lovelier even than Miss Julia

a true savior
between the milky walls
of confinement

Doc, her eyes
I saw truth in them
a real life seraph,

I think she might
save us

I think she might
save us all

Emeline

Pitezel was right about this angel,
golden hair, blazing eyes
pouting lips, eyelashes
fluttering like butterfly wings

all it took to entice her here
was a promise of adventure
double the pay of Keeley's madhouse
and a striking description
of life in an energetic city

the angel came to Chicago,
came to my castle
smiled at my advances
cradled my gift of flowers
beamed at the expensive dinners
danced in the moonlight
rode side-by-side with me
on bicycle tours,
breathed in the crisp scenery

flower-flesh girl,
a rare delicacy in a time
where women are becoming hardened
by work and business and education
Emeline remains soft, supple,
pliant to my hands around her waist,
open to my lips covering her own

I don't think about Julia,
Or Myrta, or Clara

I think about keeping her
just a little longer
the lure of her grows
undeniably strong
within my pounding head

she is in love with me
my shadows cannot reach her
for they are not exposed as shadows
just yet,

she swallows my lies like honey
believes I am the son of an English lord

that we will marry and honeymoon in Europe
perhaps even settle there,

and oh my dear Emeline,
these secrets we must keep,
you shining crystal,
you beam of light
against the coal-clouded skies
how I smile at you,
how you melt against me

your beautiful tongue
hungry for love

your beautiful fate
is almost here

Endgame

Dear sister,

I am to be married to a fine gentlemen
someone with wealth and generosity
kindness and determination
the bluest eyes I have ever seen
a secret past, ambitious future

yes, my dearest sister
I know such love seems
quick as burning a paper to ash,
but here in Chicago
I have met my endgame,

here in Chicago,
I have met my fate.

Yours,
Emeline

The Vault

Emeline, love, come here,
fetch me the sheet
of this month's finances,
won't you, darling?

Yes, there, back in the vault,
but take your shoes off first, please
I'd hate for those heels to scuff
the bottom of something so pristine,

all the way back, there you go.
we must keep these things private,
you see, we must keep these things
confidential.

The heavy door swings shut,
the lock spins,
a muffled gasp.

He presses his ear against the cold,
steel door, holds his breath
listens as she inhales dread
swallows darkness and terror
regurgitates it all back up
into primal, jagged fear,

how she cries
how he hardens
imagines thrusting into
all that sentient hysteria

how she panics
how he could do this
for hours

as the air runs thin
as she panics herself
to death.

Compendium of Dying Breaths

The quiet after Emeline
disappears from this life
does not disturb
the man who played reaper

his time fattens
with new schemes,
plots to pluck money
from each fool he charms

but in those quiet hours of dawn,
he reads the continuing newspaper
articles of the man called Ripper,
cravings take hold, breeding famished
need within his abdomen's depths

extending upward
like a snake unhinging its jaws
asking the sky and earth
for sustenance, for sensational
powers as the fangs snap down
incapacitate the mouse

how tasty it becomes
to acquire another human's
last moments,
add more dying breaths
into his memory's collections

anticipation of the hunt
never wanes in its arousal
never stops bursting with flavor
as long as the pursuit lasts,
and oh, how it sparks against
the tongue
energizes cravings,
heats the body with bolted torrents

transforms the quiet
into a serenity
of tight muffled gasps,

the reaper comes again.

Chicago: Part II

"Yet, so it is, and it furnishes a very striking illustration of the vagaries in which the human mind will, under certain circumstances, indulge; in comparison with which the seeking of buried treasure at the rainbow's end, the delusions of the exponents of perpetual motion or the dreams of the haschisch fiend are sanity itself."

–Herman W. Mudgett (alias H.H. Holmes), *Holmes' Own Story*, 1895

The Devil's Dreamland

How does the Devil dream?

In soot-tinted, skyscraper tall clouds
polluted with gothic maladies of the damned

he conjures up the acerbic blueprints
rotating counterclockwise within
his labyrinthine mind
constructing philosophies made of blood-thread
warped into a web where contorted
passageways and secret chambers
fester like a breeding ground of silken torture

from the outside, the fortress's dead space
seems something akin to normal,
a turreted roof overlooks Jackson Park,
street-level shops line the ground floor,
columns and designs mesh well with
Englewood's surroundings
hiding the inner den of horror,

double-sided closets adjoin rooms,
bodies stashed between the doors
asbestos-lined walls padded into
soundproof spaces to muffle
the throaty, feral screams
he plans to elicit from expiring mouths

sliding wall panels leading down
slipshod hallways where gas jets
produce light that only reaches so far
into the dark, pocketed corners of his maze
intending to lose you somewhere
among uneven, veering halls,
narrow and curved,
doors that only lock from the outside
dead ends and stairs leading to nowhere

trapdoors and a greased-up chute
ready to propel victims down into
his ultimate paradise,
the basement cellar
dimly lit, and with heavy, earthen air
large zinc tank, vats spread around
meant to store corrosive materials,

acid and quicklime

a table for dissection gleaming
beside the surgeon's cabinet
stocked full of shining instruments
near the torture rack, sharpened
and waiting to pierce through your skin

in his underground theater of dissection,
nothing is wasted,
in the city of Chicago,
nothing is wasted

acid eats flesh off bones
every skeleton waiting,
articulation for the sake of culture
all easily sold
hair taken for wigs
clothes donated to asylum patients

you were never anything but
a delicious memory inside
the devil's dreamland

this building, so innocent at first
breathing and imagining greatness
where doors opened to welcome
weary travelers

such warmth was choked out
strangled into an abattoir
where he paces the halls
whistling the same low tune
over and over as he passes the doors
of guests, inviting them to see
who lingers outside in the darkness

inviting them to come play
in the place of nightmares
a house of horrors,
a chamber of dread
a murder castle

Shades of Wild Plum

The building shivers
beneath each curve of my footstep,
my home, my castle
fit for Bluebeard himself,
entwining murder and luxury
like salt and sugar
placed gently on the tongue
where each tiny grain dissolves
in a way blood never will.

From the rooftop at this late hour
Jackson Park looms in the gray
distance, the clip-clopping of horses
echo around as the coal-filled air
plumes darkness into the world,
the park remains beautiful even as
construction for the World's Fair
transforms this great city
into something new,
into something unimaginable.

I have been dreaming in shades
of wild plum, walking between black
trees lining a barren landscape,
when the devil whispers to me
from between those bare, sharpened
branches that look more and more like teeth,
he tells me to use the great fair
for my becoming, my transformation
into something new,
into something unimaginable.

World's Columbian Exposition (Chicago World's Fair)

1893, we celebrate the 400th anniversary
of the barbaric slaughtering
Christopher Columbus brought
unto a new world,
but you will find no anger
toward his history here
as the fairgrounds take form, as visitors
flock in droves to taste the excitement
flickering in the air like pixie dust

People keep dying,
workers falling from buildings
accidents in the form of skull
fractures and electrocution
all this death contained within
designing the great fair,

yet a madman paces inside
his castle, creating spaces
where supposed accidents
will swallow visitors whole

a madman forges his dreams
into piping hot realities
where his World's Fair Hotel
promises spectacular service
so very close to the fair itself

Opening Day comes upon the city
in jovial bursts of color,
mouthwatering scents of exotic
pastries and delicacies from themed
exhibits stationed around the park,
thousands of visitors holding their
breath for President Cleveland
to push a button that ignites
a hundred thousand
glowing lamps across the fields,
illuminating neoclassical figures,
the work of men named Tesla
and Westinghouse

Dr. Holmes turns away men at the door,
citing reasons of already being booked
to capacity, yet the young women

stroll right in, are welcomed,
intoxicated by their own freedom
blushing at the handsome doctor
who offers great prices,
who offers warm touches

they do not see how excitement alerts
trembles into his fingertips,
eager to taste innocence, summon
screeches from their tender tracheas
lick away saccharine death from dying lips,
listen to the snapping of a windpipe,

hungry to snuff out light from
wide eyes,
hungry to cut the lights open,
sever the heart to see how it beats
beneath such fine skin,
glowing like the thousand lamps
across the enchanted fairgrounds

Minnie

I find myself in need of a new secretary, and this Minnie Williams, well, she's no Emeline, no fresh, blonde, breeze of summer air, no golden lick of lemonade skin, but there is money involved. There is a fortune to be made, to be had, to consume, and I can play the part of seducer, even to this plump, baby-faced, mousy woman. Dear Minnie, dear heiress to a substantial fortune, how I feel for the tragedy in your life, how I feel the thrill of courtship in the air, how love can soothe and devastate you all at once. Yes, my dear, sign that pesky property in Texas over to me, let me take care of it, let me take care of you. Fold yourself into my arms, hide here from the cruelties of the world. I can take all the pain away. I can spin your sadness into gold.

Performance Piece

Harry, I call him, my husband-to-be,
my doctor with kind eyes,
igniting moonbeams of romance
through my heart like silver skeins
threading between our bodies

yet, he thinks I am simple
mundanely complicit in such scheming,
if he is the kind of man to launder
money and promise me dreams,

then I will hunker down
in darkness with him,
I will crunch cockroaches
running through the hotel
beneath my heels,
grind their sticky fluid
into the carpet, imprinting my mark
castrating myself from morals
within this shoddy place of affairs,
I save myself
from an eternity of stenography
like so many women I know,
happy to be fed from the greasy fingertips
of men like him, but not I,

if a sham is what it takes,
I will play the actress
because I miss the stage
and long to get back to red
curtain nights,

I know you, my doctor

who will scam who
when this game ends us,
who will take the final
bow on your bleeding stage?

Sisters

Two for one,
that's just fine

didn't count on Minnie
having such a close
relation

didn't count on anyone
becoming suspicious
when I kill her

yes, dear Minnie,
write your sister,
invite her to stay

Anna, what a lovely name
she possesses,
how it pushes on my tongue
like a divine prayer,

the fair is just beginning
and such sights await,
I have much
to show you both
and so little time

Scarlet Siege

Insanity splits through the air
like a serrated knife cleaving
melons in half, juice pools out,
lightly blood-tinged, flowing into
the mob mentality of fair-goers
flies stick to the glistening liquid
churning out tiny spawn to harvest
inside the mind of crowds

stop and sample the new
flavors of candies,
watch in awe as Tesla
sparks electric excitement,
conducting lightning through
his body like a melody,
marvel at the Ferris Wheel,
that monstrosity of a ride
hovering between adrenaline
and a drop straight down to skull-
cracking fear

within the White City's celebration,
the water stays pure, the air cool,
horrors belong on the outside
where suicides have popped up
like cherry-tinted daisies,
where horses drop dead
in the streets from exhaustion,
muzzled and blinded
they never stood a chance,

where blood runs thick enough
to brew gurgling tarns
around the great fair,
drown all the attendees
beneath a scarlet siege,
consume that split of insanity
cleave the city in half as it bleeds

In the Castle's Heart, You Die

The show of lights emerging
each night from the fair
ignite within your soul,
enticing you to stay out
just a little longer,
enjoy these inventions
that have never been
attempted before,

this is Chicago, after all
milestones are being reached,
soft cobalt illumination
surrounds lovers and friends,
courtship romances
blossom between the night's magic

when you finally retreat
back to your hotel,
where the proprietor
with his blue eyes
fine moustache
medical degree
smiles between the darkness
of hallways seeping in perfumed
reek of medicinal properties,

you become his cornered blue jay
broken wings frantic, useless fluttering
hop away to your cage,
mistake steel bars for safety
as he sneaks up behind the sliding
panel of a secret wall, quiet and savage

for you, he holds the chloroform rag
close and intimate against
your twisting body

for your neighbor last night,
he filled the room with gas
let her die in her sleep

but your body
and her body
end up together,
intertwined limbs in his cellar,

puzzle pieces of cadavers
stored in the dark castle's
never-beating heart, lost beneath
dust and uncaring hands

here, your corpse
will never again see
light shows or evening ambiance
delivered from the fair's exhibitions,
here, the doctor promises
courtship as he unbuttons your dress
sharpens the scalpel,
hardens his blade against you

anticipating that first slide
deep into your flesh
blade connecting with veins,
peeling away tissue,
caressing muscles

it goes on,
just a little longer
as he enjoys things
he has not attempted
quite like this before,

this is Chicago, after all
and milestones are being reached.

Incinerate

Their arms laced through his
a sister on each side,
aloud, he promises one marriage
in his head, he promises both
murder

Promises like fireworks
bursting overhead
the great fair's crowd
cheering as each lightning bolt
crackles with color, sizzles
against the black sky,
trying to reach heaven's gate

The reflection of brilliant light
glitters in Holmes' eyes
as he looks upon Minnie,
upon Anna,
guaranteeing both grand tastes
of wealth, travel, art, family

The initial promise
always so luxurious,
how it ruptures in motley
rainbows, mesmerizing all,
so easy to forget the ruin
hell-bent on following,
how the incinerated innards
of fireworks unspool,
rain back down on the earth,
smoked out and deceased

Delicate as every small life
watching in awe at the fair,
the sisters stationed on each side
smiling at the fireworks
tender faces radiant

Their breath catching
at the beauty

His breath catching
when each light dies

The Darkness Swallows Your Prayers

the darkness inside the vault
is total,
blinding
as if she is the first
and last
person to exist

sweat sticks her dress
heavily onto her skin
how did Mr. Holmes
not notice
her absence?

he had asked her to retrieve
the document from the vault
in the first place

Anna beats her fists
against the door
kicks at the steel,
crumples, tries one
last time to scream, to cry

her breath evacuating
her body, too hot,
too exhausted

her bladder full,
her heart slowing
total obscurity consuming
last moments of thought

praying her sister
might return to the castle,
save her

praying
this was only
an accident

Celestial

Her panic had been delicious
sweet, buttery cries for help
great, heaping sobs
melting from her mouth
onto my tongue
like strawberry cream

Each cry fills my body
with hardened heat,
stimulating every fiber,
every fluid from semen
to mucus to plasma,

How I crave her pleas,
how they wind me up
into a hungry, writhing
mess of a man

How her final gasp for air
after I flood the vault
with the gas jets
releases my straining ache,

I could do this
Forever

Anna, I whisper to the dead
quiet of the vault,
her name pushing against my tongue,
divine as a prayer

Serenade to a Corpse

Come, dear Minnie
get ready for dinner
your sister is waiting,

yes, the property
is all in order now
and your inherited land
is now our inherited land,
my sweet wife-to-be

yes, that dress looks stunning,
have I mentioned how dear
I find your sister?
How divine?

Let me take you to join her,
let me ease all your worries

shh, darling, don't struggle
breathe in deep
this will put you to sleep now

I'll be careful with your corpse,
I'll tuck you in gently
sing you a chloroform lullaby
as your skin chills
beneath my fingertips

Curtain Call

Pressure, at first. A heavy drape falling after the play ends, after I, the final
actor, bows, undresses, takes off my face, takes off the pretense.
Too many young women are missing from my city's streets.
Too many creditors and lawyers outside my building's doors.
I have built this pressure up. I have become a glutton of thievery and death.
Alone.

Pressure, at first. And then I breathe. When the great fair ends, when the banks
come knocking, when the families of dead girls show up,
when the White City has its throat cut and bleeds black, noxious sludge that
sprays
forth violence into the air like poisoned arterial spray,
I will already be gone.

Decay arrives, as it always does.
A horse carcass beside an overturned carriage.
Drunkards, convicts, whores all face down in alleyways.
Conglomeration of the dead, of newly branded filth, of something analogous
to freedom
in the color of oblivion,
but I run on starved feet, still in need of more.

Always hungry, always under the pressure
of expectations, outlined in gentlemanly tongues as the curtain rises again,
as eyes bulge through spectacles, letting glass shards perforate through nerves
in an attempt to catch me before the encore summons more, more, more.

I am already gone.

Pursuit

"Horror and fatality have been stalking abroad in all ages."

-Edgar Allan Poe, "Metzengerstein"

One Last Scheme

My time in Chicago
is drawing to a close

you cannot keep a good conman
in one place forever

listen to me, Ben,
my comrade, my trusted friend

we're going to fake your death
split the life insurance
roll in the riches
laugh at this city left behind
in soot and coal and reek
of animal corpses in the street

this won't be easy, so you must trust me
with your life,
with your children,

I'll take care of you
I'll take care of everything

Georgiana

Unplanned, as love so often goes
another young blonde, another body
for his hands to caress
for his bewitching promises
to climb into her lovely mouth,
silken and sweet

Her eyes, owlishly large,
others call it a distortion
Holmes finds the grave eyes
appealing, and
his strange eyes
look into her strange eyes,
together, beautiful
deformities melt
into background static

The wedding is set for winter,
she will be graced with the title
Wife Number Three,
yet remain unaware for quite
some time, content in the arms
of her rather odd husband

not that anyone knows
what is about to unfold
after her wedding dress
is packed back up,
after the vows are exchanged
and he uses a false name
for a false marriage

lies continue to fall
from his mouth,
spun like cotton candy
wound up neatly,
dyed in bright hues

how swiftly the first
drop of rain gushes down
the darkened sky,
dissolving sugary concoctions
into sticky skeletons

Dead Girls and Money Schemes

The investigators ask Dr. Holmes
about Emeline, about the sisters
about fraudulent conspiracies
and owed debts to workers

They should be asking the castle
what have the walls observed
what have the floorboards smelled
drifting up from the cellar below,
how many bloodbath recitals
have these doors heard conducted
from behind sliding panels?

What of the vault, the kiln,
acid vats and surgical tools,
large trunks taken away
in the middle of the night?

The doctor smiles,
an easy charmer
loquacious stories
dripping endlessly
from that mouth.

The castle shudders
witness to the drugs,
sedation and seduction,
overly familiar with the way
human anatomy looks
like sliced deli meat,
raw and bare, naked piles
of flesh on the doctor's
dissection table.

When the Inferno Begins, I Light it Myself

They won't stop
letters asking
about Minnie,
Anna,
Emeline,
Julia

They won't stop
bills, debts, lawyers
money owed
money lost

lawsuits surrounding me
poisonous toadstools
springing from earth,
forcing their toxins
deep into my throat

the heat is on,
I have set fire
to my own castle
after all these years

even when I leave
with Georgiana,
with Ben Pitezel,
the fire chases

forever hungry
forever questioning
where the dead girls are
where the money has gone

where does this end?

Blood Money

With Minnie disposed of and her inherited property in Fort Worth, Texas signed over to Holmes, he takes Georgiana southward to meet up with Ben Pitezel, who is already down there with his young son, Howard.

Another town, another alias
H.H. Holmes becomes
O.C. Pratt
during his stay in Texas
during the construction
of another building

A new bride and a new life
fresh taste of embezzlement
flirting through dry air

Do not mistake hospitality
for ignorance,
do not think their eyes
are not watching you,
stranger in strange lands

The salty mix
of arrogance and panic,
my good doctor,
do not unravel that tongue
just yet
do not spill your carnage
onto the dusty ground

The arid ranch can only
absorb so much blood
before it grows weary
before it yearns
for escape

You cannot build your new home
on the shaking foundation
of murdered bones
and expect faithful sturdiness

The dead will always
betray you

No Entry, No Exit

"No Admittance" reads the sign on the almost-finished building, so close in resemblance to the now half-burned castle left behind at Sixty-Third and Wallace in Chicago. Twisted passageways, narrow halls, odd lighting, plans for a new walk-in vault, plans for quicklime vats, oil tanks, gas pipes, trap doors, steel walls, death closets, hanging rooms, a sewer close by and waiting to be fed with excrement of the dead – a recreation, a promise for a new murder temple because this is sacred, you see, the way he kneels beneath one of the 200 doors in the new building and asks the whispering demon in his head to calm down.

All these doors…and dear Holmes, are you losing it now, that taste of sanity you almost possessed? All these doors and nowhere to go, nowhere to hide, keep running, the doors keep following within these rooms that don't connect, and you can have conversations with doors all you like, but you can never predict what waits on the other side – they are coming, and they will find you. You could build a whole factory plant for massacres, split yourself into hundreds of false identities and hide behind hundreds of doors, and they will still come for you.

Oversight

Of all the crimes committed—
larceny, withholding wages
from workers
stealing property, changing names
digging up graves
murder
dissection
selling corpses
more murder,

Holmes finds himself in trouble
with Texans not taking kindly
to a horse thievery scheme
concocted by himself
and Ben Pitezel

He is making mistakes,
things are going wrong,
and there never seems
to be enough money
keeping his pockets fat

He turns to Ben,
the time has come
they will fake Ben's death
collect the insurance money
but they must leave Texas
they must do this perfectly

Holmes intends, after all,
to make a real killing
from this deal

Hollow

Trust, what a fragile,
complicated
shard of a thing

Mix the heat
of an afternoon
with too much whiskey

Believe the conniving man
you dare call *friend*
possesses your best interest
within his heart

Pass out on the chair
your last thoughts
not on your wife
nor your five children

But wondering where
the next bottle
of bourbon will come from

Hoping this defrauding
of life insurance,
faking your death,
will ease those tremors

Imbibe

The Keeley Institute did minimal good
for I find my friend quickly slipping
back down into the dregs of drink,
but then again,
he did bring me Miss Emeline,
her sweet goodness will last
forever in the serpentine coils of my mind

But dear Ben, this deal closes,
I really thought about keeping you alive,
truly, I did

Sleep now, you useless slosh
breathe in the chloroform
deep and slow,
just how the women take it
deep and slow

With the last glow of cognizance
reflected in his eyes,
cries for mercy spout from lips
interweave with quiet prayers,
a plea for the sake of his family,
but I am the only god here
erasing the light of life
from his drunk and forsaken soul

He does not stir, but I must be safe
just a little liquid chloroform
decanted down his throat,
I work his chest, pumping
the medicine down into his belly

Arrange the body slightly,
make it look like an accident
light a match, singe the skin
burn the hair
just enough
the reek of it clouds up the room

Break the benzine bottle
set the pipe and burned
match between bottle and ruined man

The drunk clearly broke the glass

lit himself up
in an explosion,
in a nearly catastrophic fire

Dear Ben never could
hold his liquor

Putrefaction

They find Ben's body
in a state of decomposition
the stench of human rot
pluming around the small
place like forgotten roadkill,

his bladder emptied, staining
through the floorboards,
face discolored, warped
watery layer between
his skin, tongue swollen
and hanging from his mouth
like a thirsty mutt,

fluids everywhere,
soaking the corpse's
clothes in piss and shit
and alcohol

Known Decay

Holmes takes Alice, one of Benjamin Pitezel's daughters, to identify the body of her father.

The money still needs collected,
the body still needs identified

Come now, Alice
he's already been exhumed
they're waiting on us now

She weeps, Holmes is blank
the uncovered cadaver
is advanced in its decay,
skin turning black,
rotting from the bones

Come now, Alice
perhaps you will find comfort
in the gruesome body
the repulsive mouth,
are these not your father's teeth?

Yes, she whispers
between violent,
mounting sobs,
yes

Pawns

Not long after, Holmes takes charge of Alice's sister, Nellie, and their younger brother, Howard. Mrs. Pitezel and the baby are kept separate. He shuffles them all like pawns, leading them to believe Ben Pitezel is alive, did indeed fake his death, and that he will lead them all to reuniting with Ben soon...

People as pawn pieces
caught between his hunt for money,
between his desperate escape
from the authorities hunting him

come now children
let me take you to daddy,
all in good time

he shuffles them
masterly
from city-to-city
Indianapolis to Cincinnati
lodges separately from the children
keeps Georgiana by his side

different train cars
different hotels
a beautiful maze of confusion
the Devil's labyrinthine mind
strikes again

darkness has no boundaries
no guidelines,
breaks patterns, breaks hearts
like snapping tiny animal bones

within a creation of lulled sense,
something nearly familiar,
he sets up the chess board
the players and pieces
weakens them, extinguishes lights

sucks everything into appalling
misery where a thick evil
undoes it robes,
shows a bare body
grabs gloom by the handful,
rubs the grains against aching flesh
because evil is drawn to agony,
like a cannibal to familiar meat

hungering for shadows,
hungering for more pain
and you will never begin
to comprehend the vital
rumbles from deep inside
him, this disassociation between
man and monster
human and demon

the Devil dared dream
within this mortal man,
but finality is not sealed
quite yet

finality is just the next step
the next bloodletting

the next scream as the century churns

Howard Pitezel

Eight-years-old, delicate
aggravating, insufferable
little creature

shut up, you wretched child

The boy won't stop complaining,
letters from people looking for me
won't stop arriving
no matter where I go,
this must end

The voice rattling loose inside
my head like a dinging coin
commands it so,

and dear boy, come with me now
leave your sisters be
we'll write to your mother later

we're going to go look at a house
there's a trunk and a stove
and here now, eat your breakfast

you reluctant nuisance,
swallow it or I'll keep your nose
pinched shut

After the dinner
of eggs and cyanide,
his small chest stops breathing

I cut
and slice
and carve
the small boy
into smaller pieces

shove the bricks of flesh
into the stove
bury it with corncobs and wood

decorate the offering
in coal oil
watch it burn,

fiery heat mixed with dead
child scent
slightly soothes
that rattling, pinching scream
behind my eyes

Alice and Nellie Pitezel

Their mother and the baby,
their other sister, too
only a few blocks away
and they will never know
how close they were
to the people they loved
and missed so longingly
because their keeper,
their pawn shuffler
expertly stows them away
from one another
keeps them busy
as the great game of chase
and run continues

Alice writes a letter
to her dear momma
wondering why she
has not answered,
not wrote back,
unaware Dr. Holmes
never sends the letters

In this one,
Alice writes, "Howard
is not with us now,"
as she believes him
to be alive elsewhere
as she believes her mother
is states away
instead of minutes

Holmes moves them again,
shuffles his fleshy pawns from
Detroit to Toronto,
an edginess blooms within
the growth of his paranoia

hunter and prey interlocking
no matter where he places
the pieces on the board
no matter how many Pitezel
children he plans to murder

Sisters in Shallow Graves

There is a house on St. Vincent Street
where two young girls stand on a veranda
before their caretaker, of sorts, summons
them downstairs and into an uncomfortable,
fake-fatherly hug, a gripping of the shoulders,
like a warning they cannot process

Breakfast is served, overcooked, laced
with wolfsbane and chloroform
their sad bodies crumple at the table,
bending down like dying saplings
as if to sleep, to die,
no chance of dreaming, no nobility
in this poisoned death as the tragedies
and great sonnets would have you believe

There is only his quiet breathing,
a scuffling rhythm as he drags sisterly
corpses into a large trunk, transports
luggage down into the cellar where
shallow dirt awaits, cool and damp

Delicacy, in the way he removes their dresses,
folds each girl into the soil as if planting
forgotten seeds, but no fruit will be rooted,
only the stinking rot of pubescent flesh
flaking off into the mouths of hungry maggots

There is no pleasure in these deaths
only a driven need for survival,
in his haste he stuffs their clothes too tightly
within the chimney, and it does not burn
quite right, but he has things to do,
damn this whole Pitezel family to Hell,

He leaves behind their older clothes,
pieces of silk, scraps of paper, wooden toys,
leaves behind sisters in shallow graves
waiting to tell the story lurking within
dead bones and poisoned lungs
waiting beneath the floorboards
of the house on St. Vincent Street.

Panic, Amnesia, and a Madman's Game

Panic settles onto his tongue
small at first,
seemingly harmless as the snowflakes
surging down from the midnight blue sky

the groundwork to kill Mrs. Carrie Pitezel,
daughter Dessie, baby Wharton
has all been laid out
in the schematics of his mind,
but
panic, settles heavier
strange musings, dreams
terrorizing his mind
as if there are amends to make

he tells Carrie that Ben awaits in Montreal,
with Alice, and Nellie, and Howard
the lies pour out, stick together,
form an avalanche that threatens
to lodge deep in his throat, choke him

he must make a trip
back to New Hampshire
back to the place where
he was known as Herman Mudgett

where he will appear like an apparition
across the frozen tundra of winter
claim a story of amnesia
all these long years
to his first wife, his first child

the lies become a physical manifestation
he cannot even help from vomiting
out to everyone around him

believe nothing of what you see,
what you have heard,
what you have read

believe only
in unfinished business,
the rest of the Pitezels must die,
that is his only truth

Caught

"I have been tried for murder, convicted, sentenced, and the first step of my execution upon May seventh, namely, the reading of my death warrant, has been carried out."

–Herman W. Mudgett (alias H.H. Holmes), "Confession"

Moyamensing Prison

The man sits calmly
within the confines
of a small cell,
like a nucleus wedged
deeply inside its atom

waiting, waiting

for what?

The accusations against him
grow in intensity every day
that he is here,
writing, eating, exercising,
whispering in the mirror
touching the back of his head
as if probing
for another eye

whispering, whispering

to whom?

Desperate searches for evidence
are moving the public into uncertainty
if the police know what they're doing,
if the missing children
and their dead father,
are even missing or dead at all,

still he sits calmly,
almost thoughtfully,
and while they search for the kids
he writes,
composing an idyllic memoir,
a heart-tugging prison diary
meant to further prove innocence
to the public

waiting,
and whispering,
and writing

Earned Conviction

Happy July,
the children have been found
newspaper headline bold,
darker than my thoughts
pooling in this jail cell
and I…

"How do you explain this, Holmes?"
the investigator appears outside my room
slight hint of *conviction* in his eyes

I wonder what the headlines will
say about me now,
if my glory will be as great
as Jack the Ripper's

I remember the clarity
of his stories in those articles
how his messy evisceration of women
leaked off the pages in oozing heaps
piling up in my mind
like dismembered body parts,
floating lips and tongues
telling me, *you can do better*

and I did,
I built legacy from the ground up
capturing women with my charm
as if they were sick, vulnerable
sparrows aching for a caretaker,
and here I am, darling
your Dr. Holmes ready to ease
you into sleep, slice you open,
stitch you back up…

"Holmes?"

I smile at the investigator,
offer a row of teeth
say nothing
give him nothing

my confession must be earned
not vomited in the middle
of summer heat because bodies

have been found

we're only getting started

Evidence

Little Howard's bones found
stuck in the chimney flue,
jaw fragment, charred mass
of liver, spleen, stomach
packed too tightly
baked together, didn't burn
the way Holmes intended

At the house on St. Vincent street,
human bone uncovered
merely three feet deep
into the cellar's dirt,
Nellie's black hair shifting
her scalp off her skull,
a slippery rottenness

A woman's footprint found
upon the painted face
of the vault's door from inside
the castle where someone struggled,
desperate to escape
shoeless and suffocating
the print embedded permanently,
unable to be wiped off,
made from acids on the floor

Rib bones, skull fragments,
severed vertebrae, human
hair clogging drains,
bloody scraps of dresses,
charred shoes
carbolic acid,
pearl dress buttons,
a child's cape coat

forming a coagulation
of damning evidence
in the castle's basement
where the devil's dreamland
still invites
you to come play

Daydreams from a Jail Cell

I am remembering the beauty of Chicago,
the thick smoke of it,
how she intoxicated like the most
stunning of sunsets,
wrapped a cloak of night
around me, perfumed the air
into a miasma of coal and earth,
wilderness and steel,
honey and blood,

I miss the softness of her,
those moments where she opened up
her streets and gifted me with a new
stranger to come stay in the castle,
always young, always striking,
all that meat wrapped in pretty parcels
in need of a butcher,
honey and blood

Deliverance

humanity is filthy
crowded
endlessly pleading
for salvation,
yet when I grant
such mercy
I am sentenced
to a prison cell
white walls, dirty
flooring,
granted one
narrow window
adorned with a grate,
granted one iron door,
latticed and small
granted one mirror

where the devil speaks
to me,
where the devil recites
a promise,

the way humanity
will crumble
in its own
cesspool
of brutality

I have merely been
the beginning

Yours,
H.H. Holmes

Abandoned in this prison cell
        where all the shadows talk

Left warped within misconstrued motes
        of dust where I am mocked

They wish for my wife to abandon me
        leave me desperate for confession

But my savior from the bowels of Hell,
        grants me a new ascension

With Him, I am never alone
        and he keeps me in his flock

With Him, I am eternally yours
        in the place where shadows talk

Three Wives Dressed in Black

Clara, Myrta, Georgiana
three wives he kept alive
appearing in his cell at night

three wives dressed in black,
whispering,
do not mourn for us

he sleeps, dreams,
rolls around the jail cot
as night terrors scatter
sticky worms to inch
along inside his brain

how he tried to keep wives
hidden from one another
like butterflies inside of jars,
but they've broken out
shattered the glass
painted themselves in death's
blood, black veils across
each face, praying
for the mistresses and others
massacred by this madman.

Mourn not for us,
they whisper again
casting the face of each victim
deeper into his mind as the worms
roll loose, melding with his brain
matter, eating through clusters
of nerves, extracting the closest,
botched thing to guilt
they can find,

and three wives dressed in black
curse his name,
chant together, become adjoined
in blood and words and spit
promising to haunt him each night
until his death,
promising to haunt him each night
he spends his eternity in Hell

The Undeath of Malevolence

humiliation burns me deep
at being turned prisoner,
small death of disgrace

my weight shrinks,
skin turns sallow
deep circles beneath eyes

can't sleep, or am I asleep
now, right now, right
and left the swinging

hand of time, let me keep
my watch, tickity tick
in the dead of night

oh, the way solitude
grinds at your pores
licking sand into skin

forgery, insurance fraud,
withholding wages,
murder, murder, murder

the list goes on,
doesn't end,
I am the list the list is me

I am tickity ticking
away, burning up
only to disintegrate

small death of humanity,
they cannot kill me
cannot kill sentient evil

it lives on
and on
and on

Kymographion

Holmes breathes in slow,
carefully
measuring these last days
of air like a careful spoonful,

do not let your hands tremble
do not spill a single drop

the other man places a device,
something called *kymographion*
over the prisoner's head,
its wide, lampshade-like form
cover his eyes, his mouth
connects his temple to the recorder

measures his philosophy
his number of breaths
how he thinks, feels, loves
the machine is contemplating
as the man is contemplating

and the machine whirrs
as the man sits,
allows the inner-voice
to take over

the recording stops
has documented so little
perhaps it is broken
perhaps the man in the chair

consists of no morality
no dictation of conscience

The demon in human skin
breathes in slow,
carefully
measuring these last days
of mortality like a careful spoonful

Satanical Metamorphose

chest walls concave
protrude sickly beneath
an emaciated form
I no longer recognize as my own

the body can handle
much more than the mind
but mine is turning on itself

sexual organs shrinking up
shriveling within,
turning me into something
androgynous and alien

ashen skin, hair color fading,
my smile nothing more
than a strange, lecherous curve

the Satanical cast
put upon me since birth
weaves between my paper bones
like thread through thin webbing

I deteriorate into insanity
skull transmutes between
prominent bumps
and diminutions,
like the growth of horns

knee to heel, my legs shorten,
my arms shorten,
no humanity left inside
this telescoping body

just malevolence of distortion
eyes that look into you,
reflect only irises of the dead

no more am I a man
in solidarity,
no more am I
a man, or a who,
no more am I a human

Villain Viscera

They want my brain
after I am dead

want to pluck my insides
out like uprooting dandelions
see where seeds were planted
deep within my demon-infested
skeleton where fiendish marrow
gurgles like a blood stew

they shall not have me,
shall not splay my innards
on a slab like the creatures
I've dissected over these years

let my flesh rot
my bones deteriorate
pour cement over my grave
seal me down into Hell

back to dirt I go,
back to dirt I am

my impulses, mine alone
never belonging to you
never belonging to science

To Dream in Darkness

Another century drawing to a close
another wicked creation,
an impish progeny of your construction
has come to you, come for you

will always be lurking in the atoms
around us, inside those dark thoughts
you dare not share aloud

breathe in, breathe out
his air, your air

seedling of evil, small as a pebble
an edifice broken into jigsaw bones
the pieces will always be yours
if you choose to assemble evil

if you dare to fantasize
inside your own
devilish dreamland

The Hanging

Sensation follows
aftermath of Holmes mania
as their American Ripper,
their very own celebrity of slaughter
takes slow steps up the platform
where two priests
and a hangman wait

Death stalked the madman's handiwork,
now it stalks him here
beyond the dark aura of the murder castle,
beyond the means of any escape
his oil-slick voice could conjure

Born with the devil inside him
he will die with him inside, too

The chill of fatality haunts the spring
morning, and though he kneels
with priests, prays for unobtainable
forgiveness, he will find no salvation

only darkness as the black hood
covers his face,
only tightness as the rope
around his neck summons a reaper

The executioner adjusts the ties,

"Take your time. I am in no hurry."

The world is dark,
spectators murmur
watching, waiting,

"Goodbye,
goodbye everybody."

A white handkerchief waves,
the scaffold below his feet opens its arms
two boards shift like plates in the earth,
dropping the man five feet down
sending the fiend back to hell

The end is not quick—

he hangs there, contorted
for the longest minute
spinning like a sick ballet show
in the air, legs swaying
desperate for footing,
hands cuffed behind him,
fingers divided in a sad attempt
to hold onto something
one last time

They leave him for thirty minutes
suspended, making sure he's lifeless,
the rope digs deeper and deeper
into the flesh of the dead man's neck

After they remove the black hood,
regret sinks heavy stones
down into acidic guts

For to peer into the eyes of a killed devil
leads only to curses upon your own heart,
and there he roots with rotted branches,
extending putrid, pus-filled bugs
to scurry around your soul,

reminding you always of the evil
concealed inside yourself,
the evil whose head you cannot cover
with a black cloth,
whose mass you cannot surrender
over to the hangman.

Metempsychosis

"I am Lazarus, come from the dead,
Come back to tell you all, I shall tell you all"
-T.S. Eliot, "The Love Song of J. Alfred Prufrock"

after I am gone
remains an evil third eye

the detectives fall ill,
my prison warden
surrenders
to suicide,

freak accidents
electrocution
boilers exploding
mysterious deaths

for many who
crossed my path

for any who spit
on my unmarked grave,
slightly off the beaten path
of Lazarus Avenue

Unblessed Excavation
Holy Cross Cemetery, 2017

121 years I have slumbered
beneath a gritty dirt and concrete mixture
intended to shield my body
from the desecration
of grave robbers and greedy scientists
hungering for my brain, my heart

121 years I have allowed my bones
to root into earth,
but along came the tapping, gentle at first
enough to waken me,
enough for empty eye sockets
to peel away grime, try and witness
who has come tapping at my concrete door,
it is not Poe's raven, not his gentle beak
warning me, nevermore shall I sleep
the noise is…*you*

My fingers stretch, just bone now
crunching, popping, aching
and you,
you should have let me sleep,
should have let the devil dream inside
his concrete prison

All these dirty layers deep
where dark imaginings scheme
on their own accord
where I play inside hell's dreamland
designing nightmares
no one before me dared to envision

and
you should have let me sleep

I taste *exhumation* on my tongue
as avaricious hands steal my skull,
unearth the tatters of my necktie,
the remains of my mustache,
half-alive in the dirt as if waiting

I do not care for the way excavation tastes,
how it presses heavily on my tongue
teeth doing all the work

scraping away the bottom lip
of this mouth, my greatest ally—
my words, my charm,
the way a delicious falsehood forms

If I am to awaken, then I must taste
again the chloroformed flavors
of dead girls in my arms,
must feel the moment
when warmth leaves a body,
replaced by a stiff chill

The tapping turns to bombs
shattering concrete, bursting dirt
disemboweling my old pine coffin to dust
hands reaching,
caressing my skull,
unaware of awakened hunger

You whisper that you want to know me,
but didn't anyone ever tell you
that when the devil dreams
you best leave him alone
as he thinks of souls to reap,

Your skin,
so fair, so warm
you should have let me sleep

About the Author

Sara Tantlinger resides outside of Pittsburgh on a hill in the woods. Her other dark poetry collection, *Love For Slaughter,* was released in 2017 with Strangehouse Books. She has other poems, flash fictions, and short stories published in a number of online magazines and journals, including her Rhysling nominated poem "Dead Bride Philosophy." She is a poetry editor for the *Oddville Press*, a graduate of Seton Hill's MFA program, a member of the SFPA, and an active member of the HWA. She embraces all things strange and can be found lurking in graveyards or on Twitter @SaraJane524 and at saratantlinger.com

Made in the
USA
Middletown, DE

75800618R00073